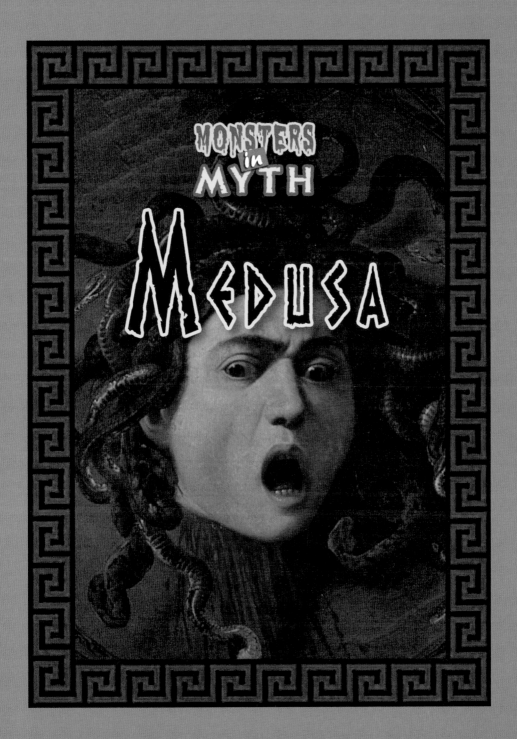

MONSTERS in MYTH

MEDUSA

MONSTERS in MYTH

TITLES IN THE SERIES

CERBERUS

THE CHIMAERA

THE CYCLOPES

THE MONSTERS OF HERCULES

MEDUSA

THE MINOTAUR

THE SIRENS

THE SPHINX

MONSTERS in MYTH

MEDUSA

KATHLEEN TRACY

Mitchell Lane
PUBLISHERS

P.O. BOX 196
HOCKESSIN, DELAWARE 19707
VISIT US ON THE WEB: WWW.MITCHELLLANE.COM
COMMENTS? EMAIL US: MITCHELLLANE@MITCHELLLANE.COM

Mitchell Lane

PUBLISHERS

Printing   1   2   3   4   5   6   7   8   9

Library of Congress Cataloging-in-Publication Data
Tracy, Kathleen.
  Medusa / by Kathleen Tracy.
      p. cm. — (Monsters in myth)
  Includes bibliographical references and index.
  ISBN 978-1-58415-928-5 (library bound)
  1. Medusa (Greek mythology)—Juvenile literature. I. Title.
  BL820.M38T73 2011
  398.20938'01—dc22
                                                                                          2010011145

ABOUT THE AUTHOR: Kathleen Tracy has been a journalist for over twenty years. Her writing has been featured in magazines including *The Toronto Star*'s "Star Week," *A&E Biography* magazine, *KidScreen*, and *TV Times*. She is also the author of over 85 books, including numerous books for Mitchell Lane Publishers, such as *The Fall of the Berlin Wall; Paul Cézanne; The Story of September 11, 2001; The Clinton View; We Visit Cuba; Johnny Depp; Mariah Carey;* and *Kelly Clarkson*. Tracy lives in the Los Angeles area with her two dogs and African Grey parrot.

AUTHOR'S NOTE: The stories retold in this book use dialogue as an aid to readability. The dialogue is based on the author's research.

PUBLISHER'S NOTE: This story is based on the author's extensive research, which she believes to be accurate. Documentation of such research is contained on page 46.

The internet sites referenced herein were active as of the publication date. Due to the fleeting nature of some web sites, we cannot guarantee they will all be active when you are reading this book.

To reflect current usage, we have chosen to use the secular era designations BCE ("before the common era") and CE ("of the common era") instead of the traditional designations BC ("before Christ") and AD (*anno Domini,* "in the year of the Lord").

TABLE OF CONTENTS

MONSTERS IN MYTH

Chapter One
Slaying a Monster.. 7
For Your Information: The Greek Pantheon................. 11

Chapter Two
The Mycenaean Age... 13
For Your Information: Ovid's *Metamorphoses* 19

Chapter Three
A Hero Is Born 21
For Your Information: Gorgons 27

Chapter Four
Confronting the Gorgons.................................... 29
For Your Information: The Helm of Hades 35

Chapter Five
Behind the Medusa Myth 37
For Your Information: Medusa in Modern Times 42

Chapter Notes 44
Chronology 45
Further Reading 46
    Books 46
    Works Consulted 46
    On the Internet 46
Glossary 47
Index 48

MEDUSA

Medusa was not born a monster. Although both her parents were deities, she was a mortal who incurred the wrath of a goddess.

MEDUSA

CHAPTER 1

Slaying a Monster

Medusa woke to the lonely sound of silence. It was quiet living at the end of the world. She got up and moved to the mouth of the cave where she and her sisters, the Gorgons, spent their days. She stared out across the island, deserted except for the stone statues that littered the landscape. Stone birds sat lifeless on tree limbs. A stone deer still had the grass it had been eating in its mouth before fatally glancing at the cave where Medusa now stood.

At least the animals looked peaceful in their poses. Medusa looked at the faces of the human statues, each frozen for eternity into a twisted mask of horror. She moved closer to one of the statues. In its stone hand was a shield. She gazed at her reflection, a sight so terrible that anyone else who looked at her turned to stone.

"There was a time," she said sadly to the statue, "when I was beautiful."

She was now covered in scales, though her skin had been soft to the touch. Instead of the snakes she now watched slithering on her head, she once had beautiful, long, golden hair and a face that rivaled Aphrodite's. It was her beauty that had been her doom—that, and Poseidon, she thought bitterly.

Medusa turned to look at the ocean in the distance. She hadn't sought out the god's attentions. She had been looking forward to getting married and starting a family. But now she never would. Athena (uh-THEE-nuh) had seen to that.

"It's not fair," she said angrily.

Poseidon had seduced *her* in the goddess' temple. She had only gone there to pray. Why wasn't he the one to get punished?

Her anger turned to resignation—the gods always forgave each other; then they made humans pay the price.

The worst part was the loneliness. Medusa's only companions now were her sisters. She missed people. She missed her old life. She was tired of men trying to kill her because she was had become a monster.

Medusa looked again at the stone statues, among them many would-be executioners. The snakes on her head hissed loudly and her expression grew even more terrifying. If she couldn't kill Poseidon, she would kill every other man who dared approach her. If the gods wanted her to be a monster, she would happily oblige them.

She turned and went back into her cave to await the next foolhardy soul who tried to defeat her. . . .

As Perseus (PER-see-us) quietly approached the darkened cave, he saw dozens of stone statues—victims of Medusa's deadly visage. Using the magic shoes given to him by the god Hermes, he rose into the air and saw the Gorgons, who were asleep. Even though he was invisible, Perseus had to fight back his fear. The Gorgons had wings and deadly claws. Two of them slept soundly and reminded Perseus of swine. But Medusa slept fitfully.

Using Athena's shield to look at Medusa, Perseus was surprised by her beauty and felt pity for her. Instead of killing her immediately, he hesitated. Then the snakes in her hair reared their heads and hissed, baring their fangs. Medusa woke up and her beauty turned monstrous. She flashed her claws and looked around, sensing Perseus' presence. Who dares to challenge me again? she thought, glancing wildly around the cave.

Keeping his eyes fixed to the mirror, Perseus walked toward Medusa. Using the sword given to him by Athena, he cut off her head with one blow. Out of the gush of blood two children of Poseidon emerged: Pegasus, the winged horse, and Chrysaor, a winged

In John Singer Sargent's painting *Perseus on Pegasus Slaying Medusa*, Perseus, wearing the wings of Hermes, rides Pegasus as he hands Athena Medusa's head.

Gorgons were frequently depicted on vase art in ancient Greece. Typically, they had wings, snakes for hair, long tongues, and in some cases, tusks.

boar. Chrysaor would later marry Oceanus and sire the three-headed giant, Geryon.

Keeping his gaze averted, Perseus wrapped Medusa's head in the goatskin bag, called a *kibisis*, given to him by Hermes (HER-meez). All the commotion woke the other Gorgons, who found Medusa dead. They immediately looked around to see who had killed her. Even though Perseus hurried out of their lair, the Gorgons could smell Medusa's blood and chased him. Hermes' winged sandals were too fast, and the Gorgons could not keep up.

The Greek Pantheon

Greek gods and goddesses

The Greek Pantheon—the group of gods in whom the ancient Greeks believed—encompassed dozens of deities, but the main ones were the Olympian gods. Each was associated with natural events, such as the sunrise or ocean storms. The Olympians were shape-shifters, able to turn themselves into animals or people at will. But generally, they lived within human-looking bodies filled with ichor (EYE-kur) instead of blood.

Just like humans, the Olympians were flawed. They suffered jealousies and insecurities and were always trying to get the better of other gods. They bickered among themselves, particularly Zeus, king of the gods, and his wife, Hera. Usually, their infighting spelled trouble for humans, who were often put in the middle of immortal disagreements.

The gods regularly interacted with humans. The male gods in particular often struck up brief romances with young, mortal women. The greatest Greek heroes, such as Jason, Perseus, Theseus, and Heracles, were fathered by gods.

The twelve Olympians and their realms were Aphrodite (love, beauty), Apollo (sun, medicine), Ares (war), Artemis (the hunt, wildlife, moon), Athena (wisdom), Demeter (agriculture), Hephaestus (fire, metalworking), Hera (marriage), Hermes (messenger of the gods), Hestia (hearth and home), Poseidon (sea, earthquakes), and Zeus (sky, lightning, ruler of the other gods).

Although Hades, the god of the dead, was the brother of Zeus and Poseidon, he was generally not considered an Olympian because he lived in the Underworld.

After the Romans conquered Greece, they absorbed the Greek pantheon into their own culture. Although the names are different—for example, Zeus became Jupiter, Ares became Mars, Aphrodite became Venus, and Heracles became Hercules—the basic stories remained the same.

Most of what we know about ancient Greek religion, which we now refer to as Greek mythology, comes from Greek and Roman literature. The main resources are Homer's *Iliad* and *Odyssey*, Hesiod's *Works and Days* and *Theogony*, Ovid's *Metamorphoses*, and dramas written by Aeschylus, Sophocles, and Euripides.

Athena was the Greek goddess of wisdom and was born fully formed directly out of Zeus' forehead. Ruled by rationality, she was also the patron goddess of military victory.

CHAPTER 2

The Mycenaean Age

The goddess responsible for turning Medusa into a Gorgon would also orchestrate her death. When the Greek hero Perseus (PUR-see-us) promised King Polydectes (pah-lee-DEK-teez) of Seriphus (SAYR-ih-fus) he would kill Medusa and bring her head back as proof, everyone believed he was going on a suicide mission. But the goddess Athena (uh-THEE-nuh) promised to help him fulfill his quest. He, in turn, would give her Medusa's head so that she could attach it to her shield.

Killing Medusa was just the first of many adventures for Perseus, but defeating the Gorgon ensured him a place among the most revered Greek heroes. And Mycenae (MY-seh-nay), the city-state he would found after his adventures, emerged as the first great Aegean city and remained the center of Greek culture for hundreds of years.

Like many mythological heroes, a real Perseus may have lived a long time ago, when history was passed down as oral tradition, hundreds of years before the Trojan War and the rise of Athens as a city-state superpower. He was among the first Greeks to settle in the Aegean and left an indelible mark on its traditions and culture. He was the father of Perses, considered the founder of the Persians. What we know of Perseus is gleaned from a few stories and histories written by the Roman poet Ovid and the Greek scholar Apollodorus of Athens nearly two millennia after his traditional date of death.

Even less is known about the earliest known settlers in what is now Greece. Archaeologists estimate they arrived in the area sometime between 3000 and 2000 BCE. They used metal tools, were farmers, and apparently lived a relatively peaceful existence. Their

language is lost to the ages, but it is believed it was not of Indo-European origin. This period on Greek history is called the Early Helladic.

What is known is that sometime around 2000 BCE, these Early Helladic people were invaded and their village sites were either abandoned or destroyed. Their conquerors were the Greeks, who quickly took control of the region and started their own settlements. These new invaders settled all the parts of what is now Greece and started settlements. This period is called the Middle Helladic period.

Unlike the Early Helladic settlers, the Greeks were not an innately peaceful people; much of their social identity was based on war and conflict. At this point in history, their leaders were essentially warrior chieftains. Because mountain ranges divide the region into many small valleys, the Greeks developed independent communities, and by 1600 BCE, during the late Bronze Age, Mycenae emerged as the center of Greek power.

Mycenae was located on top of a rocky hill on the Peloponnese peninsula, which was then called Arcadia. It was about 90 miles from Athens, which was then a small settlement without much cultural or economic influence. Because of the arid, hot, and rocky terrain of the Greek countryside, agriculture was primarily limited to olive and grapes. Those who lived on the Mediterranean coast ate mostly fish and other seafood. Having limited natural resources, the Mycenaeans established a trade relationship with the Minoans.

The Minoan civilization evolved on the island of Crete around 2000 BCE. A peaceful people, they were skilled sailors and successful merchants. Being an island culture, they revered the sea, so the sea god Poseidon was very important to them. They also honored the bull, which was a symbol of strength. One of the Minoans' favorite sports was bull-leaping, where young athletes would grab onto a bull's horns and flip themselves over the animal.

According to Greek lore, Perseus founded Mycenae around 1650 BCE. The city-state, which had a strong navy, dominated Greece from around 1400 to 1100 BCE. According to Homer's *Iliad*, Mycenae participated in the Trojan War, led by King Agamemnon.

The most famous ruler of Crete was King Minos—though many historians believe that the word *minos* was just another term for *king*. There could have been many Minoses, just as there were many pharaohs who ruled Egypt or many emperors who led China. However, stories of King Minos endure, and it is after him the culture was named.

In 1700 BCE, a powerful earthquake struck Crete, destroying all the royal palaces. The Minoans rebuilt theirs quickly and made them even bigger. The largest and most famous palace was located in Knossos (NOH-sus), the Minoans' greatest city. The building was architecturally advanced for its time, and the king and queen enjoyed bathtubs, toilets, and running water.

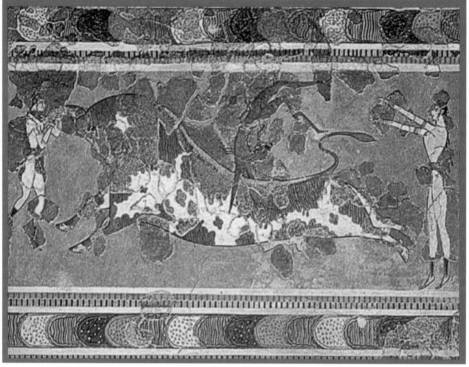

The Minoans revered sports and built the earliest known sports arenas. One of their more popular events was "bull-leaping," where a man – or woman – would somersault over a charging bull. The game had high stakes; failure usually resulted in injury or death.

Thanks to their relationship with the Minoans, Mycenae became the dominant Greek city-state, which is why the Late Helladic is called the Mycenaean Age. Other city-states included Argos, Corinth, and Sparta, along with smaller settlements like Athens and Thebes.

From archaeological digs and recovered written records it is possible to piece together a general picture of Mycenean society. Mycenaean cities were built around palaces surrounded by thick walls called acropolises. Its king had an administration, somewhat like the U.S. president has a Cabinet. While the king amassed wealth, most of the citizens lived modestly. It was a culture where hunting was more popular than artistic pursuits. Their economy was based on trade and conquering.

For over four centuries the Mycenaeans would rule the Aegean region, largely through intimidation and conflict. It is believed the Minoan civilization, which thrived until around 1450 BCE, was conquered by the Mycenaeans, around the time the other Greek city-states began to grow into more powerful cultures. Among the evidence of a Mycenaen takeover is that after 1500 BCE, their written language, called Linear B, started to dominate Cretan records. Also, the Olympic gods from classic Greek mythology evolved from a mingling of Mycenaean and Minoan gods and goddesses. All the renowned palaces were destroyed by fire except for the great palace of Knossos.

The most famous Mycenaean conflict was against Troy, a very wealthy city located on the coast of Asia Minor. The war was recounted hundreds of years later in Homer's two epic poems, *Iliad* and *Odyssey*. Homer's work was long considered to be fiction until 1870, when archaeologist Heinrich Schliemann, using geographical clues gleaned from Homer, identified the city of Troy in Turkey. He also later located and excavated the cities of Mycenae and Tiryns. Homer's poems helped identify historical locations two thousand years after they were written.

Not long after they destroyed Troy, when they should have been at their most powerful, the Mycenaeans vanished from the historical record over the course of just a hundred years. Beginning around 1200 BCE, there was a dramatic exodus from their cities, which were abandoned by 1100 BCE. Later Greeks believed that the Mycenaeans were overrun by the Dorians, a comparatively less civilized Greek-speaking culture that migrated down from northern Greece.

Unlike the Mycenaeans, the Dorians were a peaceful, agricultural people who lived a more tribal existence in small villages. The Dorians did not leave a written history, so this period of the region's history is call the Greek Dark Ages or Greek Middle Ages. It lasted until approximately 750 BCE—right around the time of Homer's *Iliad* and *Odyssey*.

Living on an island, Minoan culture was closely tied to the sea. Some archaeologists theorize it may have been the sea that caused its ultimate ruin. North of Crete is the island of Thera. Around 1500 or 1600 BCE, a volcano on the island named Santorini erupted, destroying a third of Crete and covering it with ash. Some believe it may have caused a 300-foot tsunami to hit the island, a calamity that would have spelled Crete's doom.

Even though Greek gods were believed to have power over all aspects of earth, they were also human-like in that they exhibited human traits, both good and bad. Nowhere is this view more evident than in Homer's work, which shows how the vanity of the gods was responsible for starting the Trojan War. The *Iliad* and *Odyssey* also show the importance of heroes in Greek culture. Heroes were imbued with superhuman qualities and abilities. Some heroes, like Perseus, were half human and half god; others were humans assisted by the gods. Some are more than likely fictional, but many are loosely based on actual figures important in Greek history.

The four most important Greek heroes are Heracles, the world's strongest man; Theseus, the founder of Athens and slayer of the Minotaur; Jason, who led the Argonauts; and Perseus, the founder of Mycenae and slayer of Medusa.

Ovid's *Metamorphoses*

Much of what we know about classical myths comes from the Roman poet Ovid. His epic poem *Metamorphoses* retells around 250 myths, including the story of Medusa. A prolific writer, Ovid influenced some of the world's greatest literary figures, including Shakespeare and Chaucer.

Publius Ovidius Naso, or Ovid, was born in 43 BCE in Sulmona, a community about 100 miles east of Rome. The region's main industries were growing corn and grapes. Ovid also mentioned the region's notoriously cold winters.

Ovid grew up in an affluent family. His father sent him and his brother to study oration in Rome, considered a necessary course for a career in law. But after his brother died at the age of twenty, Ovid opted against life as a lawyer. He chose instead to follow his creative interests and used his communication skills to write poetry—a decision that made his father extremely unhappy. Ovid's personal life was also one of steady upheaval. By the time he reached thirty, he was on his third marriage. He sired only one child, a daughter, in the three marriages.

By the standards of the time, Ovid was a well-known writer. Several collections of his work were published, including an account of the tragedy of Medea.

Ovid completed *Metamorphoses* in 8 CE. The epic poem is grouped into 15 books, in which he recounts myths involving the transformation of humans into other objects. The poem, which includes Greek and Roman myths, begins with the creation of the universe and ends with the deification of Julius Caesar in 42 BCE.

Around the time he completed the project, Ovid was exiled from Rome by Augustus, for reasons that remain vague. He settled in Tomis on the Black Sea in what is modern-day Romania. It is believed that he died in 18 CE. Among Roman

writers, only Virgil has left a legacy as vibrant. In addition to leaving an encyclopedia of myths, Ovid gave scholars an intriguing, unique look into Roman life during the time of Augustus.

Echo and Narcissus, painted by John William Waterhouse, 1903

Scylla and Charybdis were monsters who lived on opposite ends of the Strait of Messina, which flows between Italy and the island of Sicily. Both monsters were originally sea nymphs who offended the gods. Scylla was turned into a six-headed beast that ate sailors, and Charybdis was transformed into a deadly whirlpool. In this illustration, Scylla is represented as a rock formation.

MEDUSA

CHAPTER 3

A Hero Is Born

From the ancient Greeks' perspective, the world was a dangerous and scary place, no place more so than the sea. The deep, cold waters were home to deadly, mysterious creatures. Although sharks are now effectively extinct in the Mediterranean Sea, three thousand years ago great whites, hammerheads, and many other species were plentiful. The Greeks very much believed in monsters and usually blamed the gods for their existence.

Not all Greek gods were created equal. While the best known are the Olympian gods, there were hundreds of others. According to Greek theology, the time before the creation of the universe was called Chaos. Out of the Chaos came Gaia (GUY-uh), the personification of Earth—the ancient Greek version of Mother Earth. Through parthenogenesis, Gaia produced Ouranos (OOR-uh-nus, the sky), Ourea (OOR-ee-uh, the mountains), and Pontus (the sea).

With Ouranos, Gaia bore the Cyclopes (SIE-kloh-peez) and the Titans, among others. Her mating with Ouranos resulted in the heavenly gods. With Pontus she gave birth to several seas gods, including Ceto (KEE-toh) and Phorcys (FOR-sis), who were the gods of large sea creatures.

Phorcys also presided over the hidden dangers in the sea. He married his sister Ceto and they had several children together, many of them monsters, such as Scylla (SKIH-lah), who ate sailors; Ladon, a hundred-headed sea-serpent; the sea foam spirits; the Graeae (GRY-eye); and the Gorgons.

There are several different depictions of Gorgons in ancient Greek literature, but the most common is that there were three Gorgon sisters. Two of them—Stheno and Euryale—were immortal. They

had the skin of a lizard and snakes for hair. They were so physically hideous that anyone who looked at them turned to stone. The Greeks believed the Gorgons were responsible for the reefs that frequently damaged or sank ships.

Medusa, however, was born a mortal and was known for her beauty and luxurious hair. Poseidon, the god of the sea, became enamored with her and her golden hair after seeing her praying in one of Athena's temples. He disguised himself as a horse and forced himself upon her. The goddess was furious that Poseidon and Medusa used one of her temples for a liaison. Since there wasn't much she could do to Poseidon, she took her anger out on Medusa. Athena knew that Medusa had been vain about her looks, so she turned her into a monster, just like her sisters. Medusa's hair grew snakes, her tongue became black and grew too large to fit in her mouth, and her hands transformed into claws.

The blood of Medusa and her sisters had special powers. Blood from the Gorgons' right side could bring the dead back to life. Blood from the monsters' left side was a deadly poison. Medusa, who lived near the entrance to the Underworld, became known throughout the land as a fearsome monster to be avoided at all cost. Those who came too close never returned—until a young warrior named Perseus showed up on a mission to kill.

Slaying monsters is one of the things that set a Greek hero apart from average mortal men. Heracles had to defeat many monsters,

Poseidon

including the Hydra, a many-headed, teeth-gnashing swamp creature. Theseus was pitted against the Minotaur—a human-eater with the head of a bull and the body of a man. But at least when Heracles and Theseus fought their adversaries, they could see what they were doing. Perseus had to defeat his opponent without being able to look at it. Medusa the Gorgon was a monster so hideous that a single glance turned men to stone.

The story of Perseus begins with his grandfather, King Acrisius (ah-KRIH-see-us) of Argos, and his twin, Proteus (PROH-tee-us). The two brothers were supposed to rule Argos together, but each tried to steal the other's share of the kingdom. A battle ensued, and when Acrisius won, he drove Proteus out of Argos. Proteus eventually came back with a new wife and an army of Cyclopes. The brothers finally agreed that Acrisius would rule Argos and Proteus would rule the nearby city of Tiryns.

Acrisius was married to Aganippe (uh-GAN-ih-pee) and they had one child, a daughter named Danaë (duh-NYE). Acrisius wanted a male heir and consulted a seer to ask if that was in his future. Instead the king received shocking news. Not only would he never have a son, but the gods would punish him for raising arms against his brother for personal gain. The oracle revealed that a grandson born to Danaë would kill the king. Rather than repent and ask for the gods' mercy, Acrisius imprisoned Danaë in an underground cell lined with brass so that nobody could find her—or make her a mother.

Acrisius underestimated the gods. Zeus visited Danaë in the form of a golden shower, which was able to get into her enclosure. She gave birth to a son she named Perseus. When Acrisius learned his daughter had given birth, he stuffed her and the baby into a wooden chest and threw it into the Aegean Sea.

Again, Zeus thwarted Acrisius. He guided the chest safely to the island of Seriphus (SAYR-ih-fus), which was ruled by King Polydectes (pah-lee-DEK-teez). His brother Dictys (DIK-tis) was a poor

Danaë and the Shower of Gold, painted by Titian, 1554. Zeus sired Perseus when he seduced Danaë disguised as a golden rain shower.

fisherman. Just like Acrisius and Proteus, Polydectes and Dictys did not get along.

One day Dictys caught the chest in his net and discovered it held a young woman and her baby. Danaë told him how her father was trying to kill Perseus. To protect them, Dictys told people Danaë and Perseus were distant relatives and let them move into his house. Dictys and his wife had no children, so they grew to love Danaë and Perseus like a daughter and grandson.

When Perseus was fifteen he began working as a sailor on merchant ships. Tall, athletic, brave, and handsome, it was easy to see he was part god.

Acrisius Casts Danaë and Perseus into the Sea, painted by William Russell Flint, 1931.
Danaë and her son, Perseus, were rescued by Dictys and taken to the island of Seriphus.
Dictys took them in and raised Perseus as a son.

Perseus would become a cunning hero who was favored by the gods.

Their peaceful existence was threatened when Dictys' brother, King Polydectes, became enamored with Danaë. She spurned his romantic advances, which enraged the king. While Perseus was away on a voyage, Polydectes kidnapped Danaë from his brother's house—since she wouldn't live with Polydectes as a wife, he made her his slave.

Polydectes' tyranny set into motion the events that would turn Perseus into a legendary Greek hero.

Gorgons

Gorgon mask

Gorgons are mentioned in some of the earliest known Greek writings, including those of Homer.

About her shoulders she flung the taselled aegis, fraught with terror . . . and therein is the head of the dread monster, the Gorgon, dread and awful, a portent of Zeus that beareth the aegis.[1]

In his epic poem *Theogony,* Hesiod describes Medusa as mortal and her two sisters, Stheno and Euryale, as immortal. He also identifies them as daughters of Phorcys and sisters of the Graeae (or Graiae).

To Phorcys Ceto bore the fair-cheeked Graiae . . . then the Gorgons, who dwell beyond glorious Okeanos, at earth's end, toward night, by the clear-voiced Hesperides, Stheno, Euryale, and ill-fated Medusa who was mortal; the other two were ageless and immortal.[2]

The word *gorgon* comes from the Greek word *gorgos,* which means "terrible." And indeed it is the Gorgons' appearance that generated the most comment from ancient writers, dramatists, and artists. With the notable exception of Medusa, Gorgons are depicted as hideous monsters. Some paintings show them with long, black tongues and huge teeth. Instead of hair they possess a head full of living poisonous snakes, and they have scales instead of skin. In most written descriptions, the Gorgons are said to have claws for hands, razor-sharp fangs, and wings of gold.

Medusa, however, doesn't always follow the traditional Gorgon model. While she is sometimes referred to as a hideous monster like her sisters, she is just as often described as a beautiful woman who just happens to have snakes for hair and a gaze that turns men to stone.

The power of the Gorgon to turn people to stone could be a handy weapon against enemies. It was believed that ancient oracles, or seers, protected their temples with the image of a Gorgon.

The Call of Perseus, painted by Sir Edward Burne-Jones, 1876. When Perseus was away working on a ship, Athena came to him in a dream. Throughout his life, she would remain one of Perseus' biggest supporters.

MEDUSA

CHAPTER 4

Confronting the Gorgons

Unaware that his mother was being held prisoner, Perseus happily lived the life of a sailor. One day while his ship was anchored at the small island of Samos (SAH-mohs), Perseus took a nap in the woods. He dreamed that an extremely tall, exquisitely beautiful woman with gray eyes approached him. She wore a helmet, carried a spear, and was dressed in blue robes. A goatskin was slung over one shoulder. She also carried a shield made of gleaming brass.

The woman introduced herself as the goddess Athena and asked Perseus to complete a mission for her. She wanted him to kill a monster so that she could put its head on her shield. In the depths of the shield he could see the monster. The face belonged to a beautiful woman, but instead of hair, snakes covered her head. She also had wings and claws. Athena told Perseus the monster was the Gorgon Medusa. He was more than willing to do the goddess' bidding, but she told him he was still too young. He needed to grow into a man first.

When Perseus woke up, he could not get the vision of the Medusa out of his mind. But as he returned home and discovered the king was holding his mother against her will, the monster was temporarily forgotten. He rushed to the palace and found Danaë, grinding grain and weeping. Before Perseus could take her away, Polydectes came in, furious that Perseus should defy him.

Irate at the way his mother had been treated, Perseus intended to kill Polydectes, but Danaë begged him not to. Dictys arrived and asked Perseus to spare his brother. Reluctantly, Perseus let Polydectes live and took his mother to the temple of Athena, where she would be safe from the king. Polydectes was not willing to let the matter drop, and he spent his days plotting to get Danaë back. He realized the only way to do that was to find a way to get Perseus off the island.

A short time later, Polydectes announced his engagement to Hippodameia (hih-poh-DAY-mee-uh), whose father ruled the city of Pisa. To celebrate his upcoming marriage, Polydectes hosted a banquet and announced that each guest was required to bring a gift. Perseus, a poor teenager, came empty-handed. He became ashamed and embarrassed when the other guests ridiculed him—just what Polydectes had hoped for.

In an effort to save face, the brash teenager boasted that he would bring the king a truly unique gift—the head of Medusa. Polydectes held him to his word and immediately ordered him to leave the island and not return until he brought back the Gorgon's head.

As soon as Perseus left the palace, he began having doubts over whether he could live up to his dream. He prayed to Athena, asking for her help. Once again she appeared, accompanied this time by Hermes, and told Perseus his adventure to kill Medusa would take seven years. She told him how to find the Gorgon and described her.

> Once she was a maiden as beautiful as morn, till in her pride she sinned a sin at which the sun hid his face; and from that day her hair was turned to vipers, and her hands to eagle's claws; and her heart was filled with shame and rage, and her lips with bitter venom; and her eyes became so terrible that whosoever looks on them is turned to stone; and her children are the winged horse and the giant of the golden sword; and her grandchildren are Echidna the witch-adder, and Geryon the three-headed tyrant, who feeds his herds beside the herds of hell. So she became the sister of the Gorgons, Stheino and Euryte the abhorred, the daughters of the Queen

of the Sea. Touch them not, for they are immortal; but bring me only Medusa's head.[1]

Athena gave Perseus her brass shield to use as a mirror so that he could avoid looking directly at Medusa. Hermes gave him a pair of winged sandals that enabled him to fly over the sea, a sword made of diamond that could cut through the Gorgon's scaly skin, and a bag in which to put her head once it was cut off. Before Athena left, she told Perseus that if he achieved his quest, he would be guaranteed a place on Olympus beside the gods.

Armed with his shield and sword, Perseus left the island ready to risk death in search of everlasting glory.

To find where Medusa lived, Perseus went to see the Graeae, three witches who were sisters of the Gorgons. They had been born with gray hair and had only one eye and one tooth to share among them. They lived in a cave near the ocean, which was frigidly cold.

He came to the edge of the everlasting night, where the air was full of feathers, and the soil was hard with ice; and there at last he found the three Grey Sisters, by the shore of the freezing sea, nodding upon a white log of drift-wood, beneath the cold white winter moon; and they chanted a low song together, "Why the old times were better than the new."
There was no living thing around them, not a fly, not a moss upon the rocks. Neither seal nor sea-gull dare come near, lest the ice should clutch them in its claws.[2]

Perseus approached the Graeae, and when one sister tried to pass their eye to the others so that they could see what he looked like, Perseus grabbed the eye. He threatened to throw it into the ocean if they did not tell him where to find Medusa. Having no choice, they told him.

Perseus and the Graiae, painted by Sir Edward Burne-Jones, 1892. The Graeae were three witch sisters that shared one eye.

"You must go, foolish boy, to the southward, into the ugly glare of the sun, till you come to Atlas the Giant, who holds the heaven and the earth apart. And you must ask his daughters, the Hesperides (hess-PAYR-ih-deez), who are young and foolish like yourself."[3]

Perseus left the Graeae and traveled to the mountain where Atlas stood holding up the sky. He came across some nymphs dancing in the forest and asked for directions to the Gorgon's lair. They, too, were skeptical.

Perseus and the Sea Nymphs, painted by Sir Edward Burne-Jones, 1900. The eldest niece of Atlas ventured to the Underworld to retrieve a helmet from Hades that would turn Perseus invisible.

"Fair boy, if you are bent on your own ruin, be it so. We know not the way to the Gorgon; but we will ask the giant Atlas, above upon the mountain peak, the brother of our father, the silver Evening Star. He sits aloft and sees across the ocean, and far away into the Unshapen Land."

Perseus followed the nymphs to where their uncle was kneeling as he held the heavens and the earth apart. When asked where the Gorgons lived, Atlas pointed to the ocean. "The Gorgons lie on an island far away. But Perseus can never come near them, unless he has the hat of darkness, which makes whoever wears it invisible."

"Where is that hat?" Perseus asked. "I need to find it."

Atlas smiled and shook his head. "No mortal can seek out the hat, for it resides in the depths of Hades. However, my nieces are immortal so they can get it for you. But only if you will promise me one thing and keep your faith."

He asked Perseus to come back with the head of Medusa and turn him to stone, "that I may lose my feeling and my breathing, and become a stone forever; for it is weary labor for me to hold the heavens and the earth apart," Atlas said.

Perseus promised, and the eldest nymph went into Hades and brought back the magic hat. He put it on and, disappearing from their sight, headed for the Gorgons' lair at the end of the world.

Replica of Athena's shield

The Helm of Hades

Perseus was one of many who took advantage of the invisibility granted by the Helm of Hades. When Zeus and his clan were fighting a ten-year war with the Titans, Zeus released three Cyclopes from Tartarus, the depths of the Underworld. These one-eyed craftsmen created three gifts to help the Olympians win the war: a thunderbolt for Zeus, a trident for Poseidon, and a cap of invisibility for Hades. Hades used the cap to slip into the Titans' camp and steal all their weapons. When they awoke, they had nothing with which to fight, so they surrendered. Zeus sent the Titans to Tartarus.

Hades allowed several others to use the Helm of Darkness, as it was also called. In another war of the gods, this one against the Gigantes (Giants),

Hermes donned the cap of darkness to slay one of the enemy: "Hermes, who was wearing the helmet of Haides, killed Hippolytos in the course of the battle."[4]

During the Trojan War, Athena used the cap to escape the notice of Ares. According to the *Iliad*, she climbed in a chariot with her favorite warrior Diomedes and helped him wound the god of war.

Hades holding the Helm of Darkness on a platter, detail from a Greek vase

In *The Baleful Head*, by Sir Edward Burne-Jones, painted around 1887, Perseus shows Andromeda a reflection of Medusa. On his way back to Seriphus, Perseus saved the princess Andromeda from a sea creature and married her. After Andromeda's death, Athena placed her in the sky as a constellation.

MEDUSA

CHAPTER 5

Behind the Medusa Myth

Perseus may have killed Medusa, but her lifeless head retained its deadly powers. On his way back to Seriphus on the wings of Hermes' shoes, Perseus passed over the Libyan Desert. Drops of Medusa's blood dripped from the bag. Every drop that landed on the desert sand transformed into a nest of snakes, which is why the desert is home to so many species of serpents. Perseus also kept his promise to Atlas and turned the Titan to stone by showing him Medusa's severed head.

When Perseus finally returned to Seriphus, he went to the palace. He walked into the room where Polydectes was entertaining a group of friends. The king looked up, shocked to see the young hero had returned. Perseus took great pleasure in the king's surprise and the flicker of fear in his eyes.

Looking at Polydectes enraged Perseus as he thought about the king's brutal treatment of his mother. He walked slowly toward the king, carrying the *kibisis*. The room grew quiet as everyone watched Perseus approach. His eyes met the king's, and with a quick movement, Perseus grabbed Medusa's head from the bag and held it up. The screams of the king and his friends were cut short as they turned to stone. His vengeance complete, Perseus put the Gorgon's head away and walked out.

Afterward, Perseus appointed Dictys king. He returned the goatskin bag and the winged sandals to Hermes, along with the helmet. Then he returned the shield to Athena and presented her with Medusa's head. The goddess affixed the head to her shield, giving it the power to turn her enemies to stone. The goddess who had originally

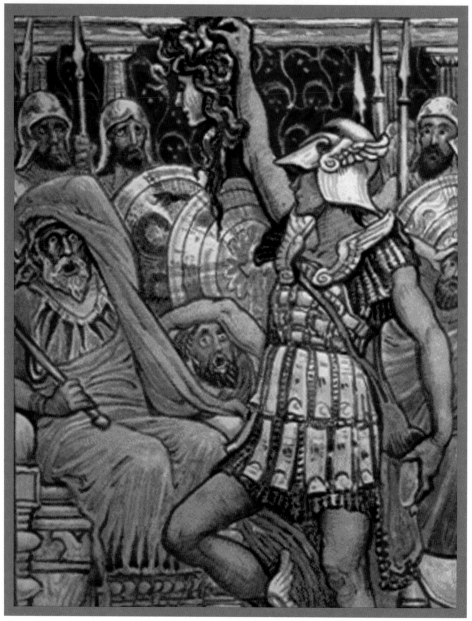

Illustration from Nathaniel Hawthorne's *A Wonder Book for Girls and Boys*, first published in 1852. Perseus delivers his promised wedding present to Polydectes.

condemned the beautiful Medusa to life as a monster now possessed her head and visage for eternity.

The origin of the Medusa myth is shrouded in mystery and uncertainty. In ancient literature she is portrayed as a symbol of anything feminine—an everywoman. The etymology of the name Medusa is subject to debate. Some suggest it is a form of the Greek word *metis,* which translates to "feminine wile" or "deception." *Medusa* also translates to "queen" or "leader." The argument has been made that the male-dominated Greek and Roman societies shared a primal fear of female power; specifically the power to create life and give birth. It was also a widely held notion that the gods created women as a punishment for men to endure.

A second-century CE Greek geographer named Pausanias describes an alleged historical event that could have served as the inspiration for the Medusa myth:

> Not far from the building in the market-place of Argos is a mound of earth, in which they say lies the head of the Gorgon Medusa. I omit the miraculous, but give the rational parts of the story about her. After the death of her father, Phorcus, she reigned over those living around Lake Tritonis, going out hunting and leading the Libyans to battle. On one such occasion, when she was encamped with an army over against the forces of Perseus, who was followed by picked troops from the Peloponnesus, she was assassinated by night. Perseus, admiring her beauty even in death, cut off her head and carried it to show the Greeks.[1]

Pausanias recounts another theory proposed by a Greek historian named Procles:

> But Procles, the son of Eucrates, a Carthaginian, thought a different account more plausible than the preceding. It is as

follows. Among the incredible monsters to be found in the Libyan desert are wild men and wild women. Procles affirmed that he had seen a man from them who had been brought to Rome. So he guessed that a woman wandered from them, reached Lake Tritonis, and harried the neighbours until Perseus killed her; Athena was supposed to have helped him in this exploit, because the people who live around Lake Tritonis are sacred to her.[2]

While snakes generally have a negative connotation in modern culture, their symbolism was more complex in Greek society. On one hand, snakes—or more specifically, their regular shedding of skin—represented nature's cycle of birth, death, and rebirth. On the other hand, snakes were seen as deceptive and never to be trusted; again, in keeping with a typical Greek man's view of women in general.

While some writers paint her as a victim of Poseidon, others suggest she brought on her fate through vanity by comparing her beauty to that of Athena's. It is typical that Medusa is blamed for being attacked by Poseidon. She is punished for attracting the god, simply for being beautiful, a reflection of the pervasive attitude that a woman's attractiveness "forces" men to act inappropriately.

Zeus

In mythological terms, Medusa was a symbol of mother earth, who posed a threat to the Olympian sky gods such as Zeus. She held the power of life and death over all creatures. By beheading her, the male gods eliminated a direct threat to their power, justify-

The Head of Medusa, by Peter Paul Rubens, painted in 1617. While there are many depictions of Medusa in classical, Renaissance paintings, ancient Greek art shows generic gorgons more than specifically Medusa.

ing and reaffirming the rightness of a male-dominated Greek, and later Roman, society.

It can be argued that modern civilization was built on the foundations laid by the ancient Greek and Roman empires. As such, the Medusa myth remains an important and fascinating glimpse into how political and cultural views of women developed in western societies—views that relegated women to second-class citizenship for much of the world's history.

Medusa in Modern Times

Other than dragons, gorgons are one of the most familiar mythological creatures in pop culture, even as far back as the Renaissance. In the sixteenth century, Medusa made an appearance in *Second Livre des Amours,* by French poet Pierre Ronsard. In 1544, Italian sculptor Benvenuto Cellini crafted a bronze statue of Perseus holding up Medusa's head, the beheaded Gorgon dead at his feet. Italian painter Michelangelo Caravaggio, who is credited with pioneering the baroque style, created two painting of Medusa in 1596 and 1597: the first was a canvass; the second was painted onto a ceremonial shield presented to Ferdinando de' Medici.

Fast forward a few hundred years to nineteenth-century Britain. In 1824, *Frankenstein* author Mary Shelley published her late husband's poem, "On the Medusa of Leonardo da Vinci in the Florentine Gallery."

Sam Worthington as Perseus

The publishing world has taken advantage of Medusa's popularity and familiarity by putting her image on the cover of many mythology books, such as Edith Hamilton's *Mythology* and *The Queen of Stone* by Keith Baker. Several editions of Bulfinch's *Mythology* have also featured Medusa's visage.

Medusa in
Modern Times

Medusa has also proven to be a good fit with video game developers. Many fantasy games, such as Karnov, CastleVania, Titan Quest, and God of War, include Medusa or a Medusa-like character.

But nowhere has Medusa been more widely used than in film and TV. One of the most famous mythological feature films is the 1981 classic *Clash of the Titans* by special effects wizard Ray Harryhaussen. He is also responsible for *Jason and the Argonauts*. Both films use stop motion animation. In *Jason*, the hero battles an army of skeletons; in *Clash* Medusa has a rattled tail and her blood turns into scorpions. The original *Clash* opted to make Medusa hideous— the character looks a bit like a charbroiled Wicked Witch of the West.

Clash of the Titans was remade for 2010. This time, producers chose to depict Medusa as attractive, so they cast Russian supermodel Natalia Vodianova, who has been called the most beautiful woman in the world. The producers of *Percy Jackson and the Olympians: The Lightning Thief* also made the choice to have a beautiful Medusa. They cast Uma Thurman, who acknowledged that the snakes on her head are computer generated. To get herself more

in the Medusa spirit, Thurman requested a flock of real snakes be brought to the set so that she could interact with them. Now that's dedication.

Uma Thurman as Medusa and Logan Lerman as Percy Jackson

Chapter 1. Slaying a Monster

1. Charles Kingsley, *From The Heroes, or Greek Fairy Tales for My Children* (Boston: Ginn & Company, 1896), http://sacred-texts.com/cla/gft/gft06.htm

Chapter 3. A Hero Is Born

1. Homer, *Iliad,* 5.735ff.
2. Hesiod, *Theogony,* 270-277.

Chapter 4. Confronting the Gorgons

1. Kingsley, Charles. *From the Heroes, or Greek Fairy Tales for My Children*, Boston: Ginn & Company, 1896. http://www.sacred-texts.com/cla/gft/gft05.htm
2. Ibid.
3. Ibid.
4. Apollodorus, The Library, 1.38.

Chapter 5. Behind the Medusa Myth

1. Pausanias, *Pausanias Description of Greece*, English Translation by W.H.S. Jones, Litt.D., and H. A. Ormerod, M.A., in 4 Volumes (Cambridge, MA: Harvard University Press; London: William Heinemann Ltd., 1918). http://www.theoi.com/Text/Pausanias1A.html
2. Ibid.

Theseus, Greek hero, slaying the Minotaur

BCE

2500	Start of the Bronze Age (estimate)
1900	Mycenae founded (estimate)
1700	Minoan civilization emerges in Crete (estimate)
1286	Heracles born
1261	Theseus, first King of Athens, born in Troezen
1183	Fall of Troy
1100	Greek Dark Ages begin at end of Heroic Age (estimate)
1000	Mayans settle in the Yucatán Peninsula (estimate)
922	Israel's King Solomon dies
800	Iron Age begins (estimate)
776	The first Olympiad takes place
753	Rome is founded
750	*Iliad* written down
490	Athens defeats an invading army of Persians at the Battle of Marathon
404	Peloponnesian War ends when Athens surrenders to Sparta
323	Alexander the Great dies
146	Rome obliterates Corinth, Greece becomes conquered territory
42	Julius Caesar is deified

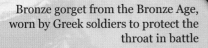

Bronze gorget from the Bronze Age,
worn by Greek soldiers to protect the
throat in battle

MEDUSA

Books

Green, Roger Lancelyn. *Tales of the Greek Heroes*. New York: Puffin Classics, 1958, 2009.

McMullan, Kate. *Myth-O-Mania: Say Cheese, Medusa!* New York: Volo, 2002.

Saunders, Nick. *Perseus and Medusa*. Milwaukee: World Almanac Library, 2007.

Storrie, Paul D., and Thomas Yeates (illustrator). *Perseus: The Hunt for Medusa's Head*. New York: Graphic Universe, 2009.

Works Consulted

Apollodorus. *The Library*. Translated by Sir James George Frazer. Loeb Classical Library Volumes 121 & 122. Cambridge, MA, Harvard University Press; London, William Heinemann Ltd., 1921. http://www.theoi.com/Text/Apollodorus1.html

Chadwick, John. *The Mycenaean World*. London: Cambridge University Press, 1976. The History Channel: *Mycenae*. http://www.history.com/search?search-field=Mycenae

Kingsley, Charles. *From the Heroes, or Greek Fairy Tales for My Children*. Boston: Ginn & Company, 1896.

Homer. *The Iliad*. Translated by Richmond Lattimore. Chicago: University of Chicago Press, 1951.

Mylonas, George E. *Mycenae and the Mycenaean Age*. Princeton, NJ: Princeton University Press, 1966.

Palmer, Leonard R. *Mycenaeans and Minoans*. New York: Alfred A. Knopf, 1963.

Pausanias. *Pausanias Description of Greece*. English translation by W.H.S. Jones, Litt. D., and H.A. Ormerod, M.A., in 4 Volumes. Cambridge, MA: Harvard University Press; London, William Heinemann Ltd., 1918.

Rand, Edward Kennard. *Ovid and His Influence*. Boston: Marshall Jones Company, 1925.

Shelmerdine, Cynthia W. "Review of Aegean Prehistory VI: The Palatial Bronze Age of the Southern and Central Greek Mainland." *American Journal of Archaeology*, Vol. 101, No. 3, July 1997.

On the Internet

Medusa and the Gorgons
    http://theoi.com/Heros/Perseus2.html

Ovid. *Metamorphoses*. Translated by Sir Samuel Garth, John Dryden
    http://classics.mit.edu/Ovid/metam.html

Perseus
    http://www.greekmythology.com/Myths/Heroes/Perseus/perseus.html

Perseus and Andromeda
    http://www.historyforkids.org/learn/greeks/index.htm

Perseus Digital Library
    http://www.perseus.tufts.edu/hopper/

aegis (EE-jis)—A shield of the gods.

deification (dee-ih-fih-KAY-shun)—The act of recognizing a person as having supreme worth; to deify, or make a god of.

exile (EK-syl)—To force someone to leave his or her country.

helm—Helmet.

kibisis (kih-BIH-suss)—A bag made from goatskin.

lair (LAYR)—A den or resting place.

merchant (MUR-chunt)—A person who buys goods in bulk and sells them to individuals.

myth (MITH)—A traditional or legendary story, often accepted as history.

nymph (NIMF)—One of the beautiful maidens that live in the forest or by a stream.

parthenogenesis (par-theh-noh-JEH-neh-sis)—Producing offspring without mating.

personification (per-sah-nih-fih-KAY-shun)—Describing something that is not human as having human or personal qualities.

serpent (SUR-pent)—A snake, especially one that is poisonous.

shield (SHEELD)—A piece of armor held on the arm that protects the body from an enemy's weapons.

tyrant (TY-runt)—In Greece, a leader who had no real legal right to rule but who forced his authority upon the populace. The term did not necessarily mean that the ruler was unjust or brutal.

PHOTO CREDITS: Cover, p. 1—Michelangelo Merisi da Caravaggio; pp. 6, 10, 12, 15, 16, 18, 20, 26—CreativeCommons; p. 9—John Singer Sargent; p. 24—Titian; p. 25—William Russell Flint; pp. 28, 32, 33, 36—Sir Edward Burne-Jones; p. 38—Nathaniel Hawthorne; p. 41—Peter Paul Rubens. Every effort has been made to locate all copyright holders of material used in this book. If any errors or omissions have occurred, corrections will be made in future editions of this book.

INDEX

Acrisius 23
Andromeda 36
Aphrodite 7, 11
Apollo 11
Apollodorus 13, 35
Ares 11
Artemis 11
Athena 11, 12, 13, 22, 28, 29, 31, 37,
  39, 40
Atlas 32, 34, 37
Chaos 21
Chrysaor 8, 10
Clash of the Titans 43
Cyclopes 21, 23, 35
Danaë 23, 24, 25, 26, 29–30, 37
Demeter 11
Dictys 24, 25, 26, 29, 37
Dorians 17
Early Greeks 13–14
Echidna 30
Geryon 10, 30
Gorgons 7–8, 10, 21–22, 27, 30, 34
Graeae 21, 27, 31–32, 34
Greek Dark Ages 17
Greek Pantheon 11, 21
Hades 11, 33, 34, 35
Harryhaussen, Ray 43
Helm of Darkness 33, 34, 35, 37
Hephaestus 11
Hera 11
Heracles (Hercules) 11, 18, 22–23
Hermes 8, 9, 10, 11, 30, 31, 35, 37
Heroes 11, 18, 22–23
Hesiod 11, 27
Hestia 11
Hippodameia 30
Homer 11, 15, 17–18, 27
Jason 11, 18
Knossos 15, 17
Late Helladic 1–16

Linear B 17
Medusa
  on Athena's shield 8, 29, 31, 37
  birth of 22
  blood of 8, 22, 37
  death of 8
  description of 6, 8, 10, 29, 30–31
  in modern culture 42–43
  parents 22
  symbolism 39–41
Metamorphoses 11, 19
Middle Helladic 14
Minoan civilization 14–15, 17
Minos 14–15
Mycenae 13, 14, 17
Olympians 11, 17, 18, 21
Ovid 11, 13, 19
Pausanias 39
Pegasus 8, 9
Percy Jackson 43
Perses 13
Perseus 13, 18, 22–24, 25, 28, 29–33,
  34, 36, 37, 38, 39
  birth of 11, 23
  killing Medusa 8, 9, 10, 39
  killing Polydectes 37, 38
Phorcys 21
Polydectes 13, 23–24, 26, 29–30, 37,
  38
Poseidon 11, 14, 22, 35, 40
Proteus 23
Roman gods 11
Schliemann, Heinrich 17
Scylla and Charybdis 20
Seriphus 13
Theseus 11, 18, 23
Tiryns 17, 23
Titans 21, 43
Trojan War 13, 15, 17, 18
Zeus 11, 23, 35